# On an Age-Old Anvil

*Wince and Sing*

# On an Age-Old Anvil

*Wince and Sing*

WALTER WANGERIN JR.

Foreword by Susanna Childress

CASCADE *Books* • Eugene, Oregon

ON AN AGE-OLD ANVIL
Wince and Sing

Cascade Books
An Imprint of Wipf and Stock Publishers
199 W. 8th Ave., Suite 3
Eugene, OR 97401

www.wipfandstock.com

PAPERBACK ISBN: 978-1-5326-5698-9
HARDCOVER ISBN: 978-1-5326-5699-6
EBOOK ISBN: 978-1-5326-5700-9

*Cataloging-in-Publication data:*

Names: Wangerin, Walter, author. | Childress, Susanna, foreword.
Title: On an age-old anvil : wince and sing / Walter Wangerin Jr. , with a foreword by Susanna Childress.
Description: Eugene, OR: Cascade Books, 2018. | Includes bibliographical references.
Identifiers: ISBN: 978-1-5326-5698-9 (paperback). | ISBN: 978-1-5326-5699-6 (hardcover). | ISBN: 978-1-5326-5700-9 (ebook).
Subjects: American literature—Poetry.
Classification: PS3573.A477 A27 2018 (print). | PS3573 (ebook).

Manufactured in the U.S.A.                                    10/15/18

Then I saw the wild geese flying
In fair formation to their bases in Inchicore,
And I knew that these wings would outwear the wings of war,
And a man's simple thoughts outlive the day's loud lying:

Don't fear, don't fear, I said to my soul.
The Bedlam of Time is an empty bucket rattled,
'Tis you who will say in the end who best battled.
Only they who fly home to God have flown at all.

"Beyond the Headlines" by Patrick Kavanagh
from *Collected Poems* (Allen Lane, 2004)
by the kind permission of the Trustees
of the Estate of the late Katherine B. Kavanagh,
through the Jonathan Williams Literary Agency.

# Contents

**Part Two: Leroy James Hopson, November 10, 1974**

# Foreword

## *A Book of Both/And*

NEARING TWENTY YEARS AGO now, I came across Ginger Andrews' *An Honest Answer*, a book that had won a major poetry award selected by another poet I admired. I remember being quietly dazzled by its simplicity, for the fragments that represented both the unpretentious and the universal, for the voice of a working-class woman—Andrews describes herself as a Sunday School teacher and a professional house cleaner—that captured the sturdy beauty of American speech in free verse. So when a review appeared shortly after, by a humanities professor at a university in New York, denouncing in precise apoplexy the state of contemporary poetry—that even though Andrews' writing exhibits how low free verse can go, free verse had debased itself as a means of artistic expression long before poor Andrews took up her pen—it registered to me as a familiar row, one pressed up against issues of supposed sophistication: hadn't Williams and Frost, among others, traded barbs on the use of form or lack thereof? And hadn't both of them transgressed their own era's snobbishness with innovation—Frost's "talking song" and Williams' hybrid verse-prose? This issue of formal versus free felt, for the era we were in, a skosh overwrought. Why, I remember wondering, is this still a *thing*? Couldn't poetry, like the vision of humanity Whitman asked us to consider so long ago, contain multitudes? It needn't contradict itself—its wildly differing forms and experiments and schools and aesthetics and manifestos coexisted, if not neatly, as a means of perpetuation. Right?

That was my first year of graduate school, when all manner of poetry came shuddering onto a horizon so gorgeous, zealous, and capricious I sat beside myself just to watch my purview shimmy: I loved Frost as much as I loved Williams, both of whom were desperately out of fashion. I loved the New Formalists and I loved the New York School. I loved Lord, Alfred Tennyson and, dang it, I loved Ginger Andrews.

Some two decades later, my preferences have surely shuffled themselves into more governable corners, though it also seems possible I'm maturing so slowly I have yet to recognize where I belong. But perhaps it's that my nascent poetic self wasn't in absolute error: those old lines aren't necessarily lines at all any more, which is to say, we don't have to either/or, do we? We can both/and, can't we? To wit, scores of contemporary poets impressively test out ghazals, villanelles, sestinas, sonnets, blank verse, syllabics, and more in their volumes of otherwise unfettered verse; in literary journals you'll regularly find poems with formal structures or their echoes. These writers, young and old and middle-aged, across the economic strata, not demonstrably liberal or conservative or moderate, they nod to stricture—some curtsy or bow. But they don't owe it to anyone. They don't perform it as an expectation. Instead, they take a kind of ownership of formal elements and make these elements labor for them in arresting and subtle ways.

Such is the delight of *On an Age-Old Anvil, Wince and Sing*. The book you now hold in your hands, this second book of poetry by Walt Wangerin, knows and blurs these lines on several levels. You'll see him working over foot and stanza, attending from poem to poem in various modes of rhythm and rhyme. In a series of carols, for instance, the meter and rhyme scheme nearly sing themselves out into the space above the page even as the content belies any lilting festivity ("The briar in a dry land grows;/ Mary will wear the bloodred rose,/ Her son will wear the thorn."). In several seasonal poems, Walt's use of anaphora—repetition at the ends of lines—creates a meditative pattern which somehow simultaneously invites you to sink in deeper and straighten to attention:

> Shoots and the small stalks sprouting green.
> Trees and the young vines leafing green.
> While scores of swallows weave the sky,
> Their beaks the needles that sew the sky,
> And fields of wheat are bowing green
> For the grace of the spacious Time between
> Is the good earth springing green.

# Foreword

The scope of the volume, in a way, mimics this lulling and startling. In terms of formal elements, the poems feel comfortably familiar even as they vary and move into unexpected modes.

But you'll find both/and beyond the mere line. Walt works over what could be seen as Victorian tendencies, exuberant theological inquiry and landscapes endowed with strong emotion, with an undoubtedly Modern terseness: over the course of this book, tonal distance dances with its forbidden cousin, earnestness; together they genuflect and titter and walk the graveyard. The very first poem offers us a fulgurant kaleidoscope of creatures and spaces waiting for the "Storm of the Lord"—". . . the salmon, / shooting from a shattered water / knows; // and the falcon, / riding the rolling, level air,/ the instant before she stoops, knows;"—steering us towards an entreaty to "call them kin," to "let these be your angels," a move so Blakeian it thrills. Pages later, it's late Eliot who comes to mind with Walt's clipped fragments—whole poems but a few lines long—and one ending here, as curt as other poems are lush: "Lent is the 'Alleluia' forsaken."

In this way (along with others I'd detail if ushering you to the poems themselves didn't seem more warranted), Walt is building a bridge, as he's been doing in his writing and his sermons and his airtime and his lectures, for years and years and years. This book asserts itself in the poetic tradition even as it insists no *one* tradition exists. Like so much of Walt's work and interaction with the world, these poems arise from a place of magnanimity, of longitude, latitude, of pluck: the poetic traditions are akin to what it means to be human—not just the one thing, many and sundry things, multitudes, erasures, synchronicities, rarities—not *either* the mystery *or* the mastery but, now and always, *both* the wincing *and* the singing.

—Susanna Childress

# PART ONE

# Six Seasons

# Mysticeti!

1.
The whale displaces ocean where she goes,
piles the element before him,
long, green marine-lights sliding down her back—
the crushing of sunlight.

And can the krill not know
what bulk approaches?
Does no fore-shock warn
their rocking economies
that God is coming?

Surely the element we swim in,
this existence,
echoes ahead
an advent.

2.
If stalking is color,
brown surrounds the cougar
prowling always
a depression of light.

Every small eye
watches from her den
contemplating the cougar
solemnly.
She veils her fear
to study survival
privately.

The cat causes the weather.
Only the fool,
when the Brown Cloud Quiet
overshadows him,
stilling the grasses at his chin,
eats
and is eaten.

3.
Listen to the tarnish of the skies.
Watch the rushing of the winds.
Taste clouds contracting to lunge.

God is coming.
God is coming,
and not one canny mammal,
mother of a small brood,
moves.

4.
But the salmon,
        shooting from a shattered water,
        knows;

and the falcon,
        riding the rolling, level air,
        the instant before she stoops, knows;

and the doe,
        lifting her face from a bank of fern,
        twisting her ears like radar dishes;

and the prairie dogs,
        standing watch on the tableland
        erect as a pepper shakers;

and the ant,
        twiddling her feelers
        in the universe;

and the hare,
        caught in the gloaming
        of the cougar;

and the krill,
        upheaving on an advent
        of ocean-water—

all these know *Kairos*
        in the terminal nerves of their beings.
        They know that the Storm of the Lord is at hand.

They long for the thunderclap of liberty,
        yearn for that bright bolt
        that will crack creation free of bondage.

All these, all these
        watch with an intensity
        of waitfulness.

They have unsullied senses.
        Call them kin.

O ye nations,
        let these be your angels.

# An Effusion

1.

        In the days of the angels—
didn't the hair of the people
stand like static?

        In the days of the angels—
didn't the air at their eardrums
crack like a solid?

        In the day when Gabriel dropped,
            discharging news in the atmosphere:
how could his electric language
not have shot their nerves?

        Skin, the abdomen,
            and deep the human womb
must have been tympanic then.

        In that day when the archangel
            uttered lightning,
wasn't the scent of the air ozone?
Didn't the air taste of seltzer and ions?

        Surely people perceived
that angels were immanent.

2.

     "A son—"
Now *there's* a bolt
to strike old Zechariah dumb,
charging the nostrils of those Jews
devout at the hour of incense
with a nitrogous excitement,
their bloods a rush of bubbles.

     "A *Son*—"
A maiden hikes her skirts and runs.
Nazareth gapes at Modesty
forking through the streets,
her knees indecently aflame,
her hair unpinned,
fuming on the wind:
"Cousin! Cousin!
I've such a thing to tell you!"

     "A *virgin's son*—"
And the father who hadn't engendered him
springs from his bed,
the bell of prophecy ringing in his ears.
Surely Galilee is stunned.
Surely Rome moans
at the impossible pop of lightning.

     "A *Savior!*"
Myriad stars in myriad spinning galaxies
plunge and explode,
*"Gloria!"* roaring,
*"Gloria in altissimis Deo!"*
The tempest of heaven shakes the mountains,
all angels in a fusillade!

     Surely no one can sleep
when the air burns blue,
singeing eyelashes.

3.
The nations smell smoke
in the morning,
oblivious that it was God
who scorched them.


4.
Last night's storm rinsed
the green leaves crystalline;
and the vineyards,
nourished by nitrogen,
produce a wine so crimson
that the drunk who raises a glass to the sun
sees a ruby in his wine.
"A toast to riches," he cries,
and swallows blood.

# Immersion

1.
The wild beast skulks midnight,
       terrifying the watchman.

The solitary traveler shrinks
       from the snarling he hears in the forest.

The carnivore
       leaps.

2.
I stand nameless in the night,
       sightless in a wilderness.

This is the speechless region,
       this is the wordless region,

this voiceless region. No sound focuses my going
       through my tar-black midnight;

no hand to map a path
       across my talus wilderness.

3.
A voice calls, "Come," and I go.
       The one who called me is a camel

blowing locusts out his nostrils,
       spitting honey in my mouth.

4.
The dawn-rain rinses me, and I,
       the unshorn, the shriven,

hear my name in the falling water:
       "Washed."

# Sacred

The wild geese lace the sky
flying north,
flying to the arctic
to lay and brood
the egg of creation.

The ancient Irishman
laying windrows with his scythe
looks up with a blue, rheumy eye.
He drops the cutting blade
and raises reverential hands.

Once It was a Dove,
the Holy Ghost descending.
Now It is the Wild Goose
flying.

# A Carol I

Mary, she blows on her knuckle—
    *The wind so cold,*
    *The night and the snow—*
Mary, she blows on her knuckle bone
While Joseph, he blows on the coal.

The donkey that bore the young mother—
    *Sing lullabies*
    *On perilous ice—*
The donkey that bore the young mother bore
The bearer of Christ the Lord.

Mary, she hasn't the ticking—
    *Stone cold the floor,*
    *The wind at the door—*
Mary, she hasn't a mattress whereon
To lay the incarnate Word.

Joseph, he sheds his warm coat—
    *Binding the hay,*
    *A cradle creating—*
Father Joseph rips his robe
Into strips to swaddle the babe.

We are the watchers who watch them—
    *Two cries in the night,*
    *Her pain, her delight—*
We are the watchers when Mary breathes
Breath in her child, and life.

We are the beasts and the angels—
    *Ba, ba,*
    *Gloria!*—
We are the hosts and the herders who cry,
"It's off to Bethlehem!"

Mary, she dandles the babe on her lap—
    *Warm in the cold,*
    *The one whom she holds*—
She counts her baby's toes,
While Joseph blows brighter the coals.

# A Carol II

*Mary, maide milde and fre,*
*Chambre of the Trinite,*
*Icrounéd and ilor. . . .*

1.
The briar in a dry land grows;
Mary will wear the bloodred rose,
       Her son will wear the thorn.

2.
Saint Joseph plucks from the cherry tree
fruit he gives to his Lady.
       Then what remains? The stones.

Saint Joseph cleaves mahogany
To make a crib—an irony;
       For Christ to old timber was born,
       To wood already worn.

One father splits two cedar beams,
"To build a house," says he.
       "To build a cross,"
       the Other mourns.

3.
Shepherds bring wool to the midnight stall:
For the mother a robe, for her darling a pall,
       His sleeping cold, hers warm.

Three gentlemen bring three measures of myrrh,
A dram to perfume, an ounce to purge,
      And a pound to embalm the Lord.

And gold is lovely to the eye,
But brutal stone to him who lies
      Inside his sepulcher.

4.
Now these, the bloodred rose, the cherry,
Wood and wool and gold does Mary
      Ponder when Christ is born.

But the stone and the pall and the briar thorn
Will wrack the flesh of her dying Lord,
      Whose body's cruciform.

The pain is his, but he is hers,
The treasure in her burgundy purse,
      By whom her womb was torn,
      *Et eius Salvator.*

# A Carol III

Whistle on wooden pipes.
       Wake the children!
       Wake the children!
Plead on the wailing reed
that the children rise up and come.

Organ! Roar forth a chord!
       Cleave their mornings!
       Open their doors!
Pour in their souls the molten
Gold of the sunrise sun.

Bugles! Bugle the news:
       "Last night, midnight,
       Stall and stable—"
Bell-bells! Declaim the good news
That a virgin has borne a son.

Bass drum! Snare drums, march
       To the rhythmic beats
       Of the children's feet,
March to the sounds of their running
That the babe can hear them come.

Gabriel, greet them now.
       *Welcome, welcome,*
       *All my children.*
Angels, ignite the sky
With the fires of an astral crown!

Orchestras! Trumpets! Choruses!
     Raise a roaring. . . .
     Children, tune your voices
To sing psalms as you know how.

# A Carol IV

Sing softly the cherries,
       Red-red, sweet, and good;
Sing apples and oranges,
       The cinnamon food.

Dance swiftly the cider,
       Spin more than you should;
Liquor and laughter
       Will lighten your mood.

Declaim the roast turkey,
       Riddle the sauce;
Potatoes are stories
       Of riches and loss.

Pipe merrily carrots,
       Drum beets till they bleed;
They root down in darkness
       Who started as seed.

Oh, candy the greetings
       You give to your guests;
The wassail is fleeting,
       And life ends in death.

So taffy your handshake
       And ginger your kiss;
Bake huggings like muffins,
       A brave Eucharist.

Be feast for our Christmas,
      And I'll be the food;
Pray Christ to assist us
      In everything good.

# Innocence

Jesus was born with animal in fur,
       Needle teeth,
       A milk-blue breath,
Four paws walking and aware—

       A natal song we sing for thee:
       *In terra canunt angeli.*

His dam with a gingham tongue licks
       All lovingly
       His sleeping eye,
Then laps her pup, his muzzle, his lips—

       Lullabies we croon for thee:
       *In terra canunt angeli.*

Thou, born of the flesh beasts,
       Ever obedient
       To thy nature,
Wast bred to host and meat our feasts—

       Astonished hymns and litanies:
       *In terra canunt angeli.*

Cub of creation, slip from thy den,
       Run among men,
       Malevolent men,
And prove what carnivores we be—

*In terra canunt angeli,*
*Et lamentantur archangeli.*

# Magi

Convulsions in the heavens
give birth to a shining word.

A newborn star, a legible star,
ascends the rim of our red horizon—

(its tail's a scepter, its nimbus coronal,
its wings a sheer-veined radiance)

—and writes on the crimson clouds, "I am!
I am the AM that caused creation,

the AM who anoints my Son
Sovereign."

# Epiphany

Signs! Signs! A thundering dove
        Descended to creation,
Himself a sign of sacred love,
        His cry a consecration:
            *"My Son, with thee*
            *Am I well pleased."*

Signs! Signs! Consignments of wine
        Surpassing sixty gallon
Revived a wedding in decline
        When lesser liquors failed them.
            *Whose was the brew?*
            *Disciples knew.*

Signs! Signs! A face inflamed
        Climbed the crown of the mountain.
Two brothers and a blowhard came,
        And the cloud cried out above them,
            *"Heed my Son,*
            *My Begotten One!"*

Signs! Signs! The world is a book
        And what is not the writing?
Nature's finger emblazons the sky
        With signs of a wild excitement:
            *Epiphanies.*
            *Epiphanies.*

# Angelus

The testimony
of the acolyte:

"When I ring the bells,
I am sound."

# Wednesday

Ashes black my brow. *Memento!*
"Remember, Mortal, thou art dust
  And to dust thou must return."

# Immured

Lent and prison
are made for the poor.

Lent is the skylark
caged.

Lent is the "Alleluia"
forsaken.

# The Owlet Moth

The naked, clear-glass lightbulb
hangs from my ceiling by a wire,
casts hard shadows against the wall,
a light too bright for my bedroom.

Out of the darkness, in through my window
flutters an erratic, nocturnal moth
adventuring the muzzy air,
the humidity thick in my bedroom.

The bulb's bright incandescence
draws the moth
who circles, circles—
until her wings touch the hot glass
and flatten like a paper plea,
her antennae crackling.

# The Sunday of the Passion

Wince, but sing.
Follow the crowd
(*"Hosanna!"*)
down the olive-mountain.

There is no mule
of such virtue,
nor one so lowly
that the Savior's sandals

drag the road
toward the Sheep Gate
of David's ancient city,
Jerusalem.

Unfold your flesh.
Cast it down before him.
Rug the road
of his passing caravan!

Now follow him through the gate.
Caper! Dance!—
until the holocaust
consumes him,
Christ, Messiah.

# The Hawk

The skeleton of a tamarack
stands one legged and singular
in a field of compacted snow.

Individual thickets hunch the hard crust.

Erect on a sheer limb of the tamarack
perches a Sharp-Shinned Hawk.
Hunger has driven her
out of her deep-wood cover.

Winter is the dead season, *this* winter lifeless,
*this* snow trackless, all the small prey burrowing,
not a sparrow, not a junco
to satisfy the Sharp-Shin's craving.

She cocks an eye. She scans the ground
of the unforthcoming, unyielding snow,
until a thicket twitches,

until a feather alerts her.
She drops—
her beak militant, her yellow eye scouring—
and on broad wings skims the snow.

The Hawk pounces!
her four-toed talons foremost.

The Hawk pounces!
She rips living flesh,
and hooks out
the pumping heart
of her sister.

# Lent

1.
If Death is the end of all we do,
all we do is futile.

We deny the death-head,
intent on this tick-instant only:

*"Here* we are!
*Now* we are!"

We philosophize mortality:
"Because we *are* we can't *not* be!"

2.
Death porches at our endings,
prepared to cancel all our days between.

Death waits to devour our denials,
and then to vomit our cadavers out.

3.
As drumbeats define the silences,
so Birth and Death,

the First and the Last,
define us too.

# The Horses of Night

Christ threatens me.
Righteousness estranges me.
The forge-fires terrify—

    *"Lente, currite noctis equi!"*

O Ghosts! At the tolling of the twelfth bell
dissolve me into dew,
my soul into a vapor—

    *Time, cease, that midnight never come. . . .*

# The Coyote

How did they kill the coyote?
They never knew.

They chased her, they raced her
on belly-treaded snowmobiles
cross-stitching her tracks.

Four men, five, on an outing.
Zipping the crusted snow of a golf-course.
Dividing and whining past the coyote.

Wind in their beards.
Laughter cracking their teeth.
Circle-whirling around the beast

whose fright
slapped her tail
between her legs.

"Damn!
Where's my rifle
when I need it?"

Five screaming machines
whizzing down a slope
like tears on mirrors.

Five men crouching and riding
in dead earnest to form
pincers ahead of the coyote.

And she, snapping her tail left
to corner right,
and right to corner left,

squeezing speed from her ribs,
squirting past the points of the pincers,
and running, her tongue blown back to her ears.

      How did they kill the coyote?
      They never knew.

that after they'd ridden their mechanical rattlers
up and over the horizon,
the coyote crack-plunged

through the snow's crust,
five feet down,
in a white pit.

Too exhausted to leap,
too feeble to claw-climb the soft walls out,
too defeated to wait another day and nourishment,

she lay down,
and the foam at her flews
froze solid.

      How did they kill the coyote?
      Like a roach in a teacup.

# The Grey Wolf

And the wolf—
how did the hunter kill the wolf?
He

froze a knife-blade
in an ice-block,
point prominent;
encircled the barb
with warm bear-grease;
set temptation
on a bare rock—

The wolf?
The wolf—
she

ran her red tongue
like a muslin
of flesh across
the grease. The taste
encouraged her.
The freeze benumbed
her tongue's thin cuts.

How did
the grey wolf die?
She

lapped blood. Blood she
tasted. Blood she
lusted. Blood she
hungered fiercely.
The her taut stomach
seized at drinking
such thick, rich blood.

> *Oh, you blesséd*
> *block of sweetblood!*

The wolf swallowed
and drained her life
with the selfsame
lacerated
organ.

Speak to me Speak
to me Speak to
me: how did the
hunter martyr
the wolf?

> Or *did* she die
> a martyr?

Could the wolf not
have known that what
she craved was her
own life's blood?

# Arising

When the turf was his tower
and the pit was his bower,
and worms prepared
to eat his eyes,

his sight became insight,
his pall the day's light,
and the worms grew wings and
flew.

# The Prophet's Mantle

1.
Sprinkle incense on burning coals.
In a column of savory smoke
sparks ascend the Temple Mount.

2.
God is the wind!
God is the whirlwind
that swept Elijah

and his four mane-flaming horses
up—until the chariot's fires
were quenched in the clouds.

3.
Ascend! O chariot, ascend!
Wheel me, wing me to meet
Messiah, the Lord of his Lord born.

# Reflections

I see thee
And I do not die.

I see me
In thine all-seeing eye.

As thou art
Life, in Life am I.

As thou art
Love, in Love am I—

In Love, in Life,
And purified.

       Alleluia.

# Peace

1.
The old moon holds the new moon
in her arm—
and shall we go to war?

"Peace," cries the prophet,
"where there is no peace!"—
and the nations go to war.

2.
But in the green season
the prince whose name is Peace
gathers galaxies in his fist,

compresses them into diamonds
harder than the callouses of the Creator,
and casts the bright stones down

as hammers and anvils
to beat gun barrels into piccolos
and canons into cups.

# Three Ecclesial Seasons and Time

The first of the first day's dawn was white,
That detonation of Time, white,
That primal word, the birth of Being,
*Fiat!* from the yawp of God,
Was a shout of Light,
Was a perfect howl of progenitive light,
>     While in between
>     The earth is springing green.

Then this will be the evening end
Of Time's long westering,
When the phenomenal noun dispredicates,
And the growl of God has closed debate,
And the western light begins to fade—
This: universal, purple gloom,
>     While in between
>     The whole earth's springing green.

And Christ's intrusion in Time was white,
When the Father re-murmured that first word, "White."
And the babe required a swaddling light.
But on that day imperial,
When the King will conjugate us all,
He'll conclude the universe withal—
>     Yet in between,
>     All in between,
>     The fields are springing green.

Shoots and the small stalks sprouting green.
Trees and the young vines leafing green.
While scores of swallows weave the sky,
Their beaks the needles that sew the sky,
And fields of wheat are bowing green,
For the grace of the spacious Time between
        Is the good earth springing green.

# Hierarchies

When the six-winged Seraphim fly to God
They burst into flames. Love is a conflagration—
    *"Holy! Holy! Holy!"*

The blue, four-winged Cherubim cry,
The guardians of the Life-Tree cry—
    *"Blessing! Honor! Glory!"*

Raphael, Uriel, Gabriel, Michael,
Thrones and Powers and I—*"Amen.
    Come, Lord Jesus, quickly."*

PART TWO

# Leroy James Hopson,
# November 10, 1974

# I.

The telephone
uncoils.
> *(rings)*

Strikes.
> *(rings)*

Satan sings at night.

"That you, Pastor?"
"Yes, Hattie."
"It's a 'mergency
down to St. Baptiste."
"I'll be there as soon as—"
> *Click!*

The line dies.
Bare feet, shod feet,
and my overcoat.

## II.

The nurse on patrol says,
"Follow,"
then quick-marches me
*(Ta-tock-a, ta-tock-a)*
down the hospital's
tessellated corridor.

(*Ta*-tock-*a:*
her heels gunshots.
My sneakers mute.)

The skin's stretched so tightly
across the bridge of her nose
that it is white.

She knocks once,
knobs open the waiting-room door,
and (apparently for my sake)
announces, "The Hopsons,"
then vanishes in a puff
of Old Dutch Cleanser.

# III.

1.
"Done took your time."
Hattie Banks is a hickory septuagenarian,
a musket liable to flash.

She wears one sweater
buttoned over two,

and a black wig so big
that if she stood she'd look
like a hall tree.

Hattie wears a pair of nylon stockings
pulled over her boots,
lest she slip on ice.

On an exhausted couch beside her
sits her niece, Mary Kingdom,
who greets me with a silken nod.

And, by Mary side,
sits her cousin Fay,
staring warily at the slender testament
and the small black box in my hand.

Beige, bare, windowless,
rectilinear, monotonous,
and unaccommodating,
this waiting room,

unfurnished, except for the couch,
a plasti-formed chair,
and a woven trashbasket in a corner.

2.
I drag the chair forward
and sit facing the women.

"Fay,"
          (*consolation*)
"I can't imagine
how hard this is for you."

Fay and impeaches the Deity:
"By-pass surgery!"

Mary Kingdom,
forever yearning to heal
every human wound, explains:

"Uncle Sonny raised Fay from itty-bitty
with a steadfast and plentiful hand."

Fay Hopson:
"Done swore he not never
gon' go under the knife."

And I:
"But he's always been a strong man, Fay.
He'll survive the surgery."

Fay, as black as Nigeria,
mutters, "Not strong. Not strong a'tall.
Sixty year an' weary."

Diffused, remembering, Fay says,
"To-mornin' him an' me
was stair-steppin' up,

when Uncle Sonny sagged,
done grabbed a-holt o' the rail
an' swayed low, low,
sayin', 'Baby girl, I'm gon'
drop an' die.'

Not strong, no.
Scared."

"Whisht."
Cocoa-colored Mary Kingdom
encircles her cousin's shoulders
with an arm like a shawl.
"Whisht."

Fay, her voice scarcely a whisper:
"An' St. Baptiste, wheelin' my uncle
to the cuttin' room,
an' me kissin' his hand,
an' him not denyin' me that."

# IV.

1.
Hickory Hattie Banks
speaks an inner-city,
sorghum-syrup dialect.

"Reverent?
(ferret-eyed)
 you ever seen Sonny Boy dance?"
"I don't—"
"Naw, you white.
Don' move in same circles."

But I *do* remember the Sunday
he sat in a pew
for Consuelo's christening:

> A luminary.
> A dapper little man
> three-pieced and roped:
> his tie carmine,
> his vest and jacket and pants
> cream-white,
> his fedora sporting
> a pink flamingo feather
> in the hatband.

And Leroy James himself,
smiling like a TV personality,
acknowledged me
with a touch to the brim of his hat.

Hattie Banks:
"Oh, he a hom-dinger,
ma brother Sonny Boy."

She unbuttons her outer sweater,
tosses it aside,
and leans forward,

chewing a story as if it were
a delicious stick of Juicy Fruit.

2.
"Him an' me always ended
a Satiday night at Fly's,
an' Fly's be jumpin' to the juke,
an' Fly's be whiffin' o' liquor and pomade."

Hattie hums the memory
in her sinuses:
"Mmm-*hmm*. Mmm-*hmm*."

Mary Kingdom's tones
tend to those of a thoughtful
Negro Spiritual.

"Sonny's a caution," she tells me.
"Well-knit, a tap-dancer
sweeter than Bojangles."

Hattie has started
to finger-tap a rhythm
on the cap of her knee.

"Sonny an' Sonny,
ma brother Sonny *Boy!*

What he do,
he push back that wire table,
then come up cock-standin'
an' *ready.*

Then it's a rush o' peoples
snatchin' back *all* o' them tables,
an' womens in they tight-ass skirts,
an' mens sloop-shouldered,
struttin' they stuff,
all o' them circlin' Fly's like they a wheel,
an' Sonny turnin' on a toe in the middle,
like Ezekiel in a wheel rollin'.

Then that slackman Tommy D shout
'Ma *man!*'
Freckled Tommy D shout
'Deal me *dead!*'

An' Sonny crack that smile,
pretty teeth white as keys
on a honkey-tonk piano.

He be *sun*-light, Sonny Boy!
An' *Jesus!*—gon' *kill* you
with that smile!"

Hattie sheds her second sweater
and her third,
an old, flat-chested woman
in gingham.

"So," she says,
"So, what I'm sayin',"
she says,
"ma brother bow
like Philip Morris,

an' skim his hat at me,
an' me cetchin' it on one finger.

Sonny slouch through first notes
of a juke-tune,
slush his foot a little,
an' peoples waitin',
mumblin' a low laugh
that go ripplin' round the room.

> *Jump an' jive!*
> *The rat's alive!*

Sonny unwind.
Sonny snap his backbone
like the spring in a clock
an' the chime.

Then he off, rollin' an' risin'
like smoke on the mountain!

> *Gonna get racy*
> *With Count Basie!*

> *Ain' no excuse;*
> *Jump that juice!*

Sonny Hopson, *ha!*—
sassiest click
of a toe-tap shoe.
Oh, them little feets,
quicker 'n crickets!"

*Sweet solid spade*
*Don' be afraid!*

"The juke drum faster,
but Sonny fastest.

He crook a knee.
He drag a foot acrosst the floor,
then *Clap!*
he up an' flyin' in Fly's!
Chatterin' them cleats,
an' them little cleats
spittin' *fire!*

It's a crowd of tipsified peoples
hoo-hawin', an' yellin',
an' Tommy D
shoutin', "You the man!"

an' Sonny sailin',
Sonny Boy poppin' his fingers,
Sonny Boy flinging' his arms
wide as Calvary,
an' damn-*dancin'*,
dancin', dancin',
dancin.'"

# V.

A knuckle-rap swings open
the waiting-room door,
framing a tall, explicit surgeon.

Fay gasps—
a wide-eyed ebony carving,
a frightened Niobe
staring at the fine spray of blood
that stipples the doctor's
pale-green apron.

He slits an eye at me,
then, as though I were rungs on a ladder,
climbs me sight-by-sight
with a cool calculation
from my sneakers to my denim shirt,
from my shirt to my unshaven face.

"Are you,"
(a professional inquisition)
"a member of the Hopson family?"

The soft-spoken Mary Kingdom answers,
"As good as family.
He's our pastor."

The surgeon observes
Fay's stark expression.
"No need," he instructs her,
"to be afraid."

So white are his eyebrows
that they appear invisible.

Miz Hattie Banks straightens
her reed-stalk spine
and starts to rock
on the unrockable couch.

The physician
addresses her.
"Accept my apology.
The procedure lasted longer
than we had expected."

Hattie chooses not
to comprehend.

To me, to the white man in the room,
The doctor states the cause.
"We had just clamped Mr. Hopson's ribs apart
when he suffered a second infarction."

Mary Kingdom's mystified.
I enlighten her:
"Another heart attack."

Bland to my interruption
the tall man continues:
"We're doing what we can.
Infusions of blood,
ten liters of oxygen,
a constant massaging
of Mr. Hopson's exposed heart."

Fay is fixed on the blood
tracking the surgeon's chest.

A small cough of conclusion
into his long, chalk-fingered hand.
"Expect," he says, "two more hours.
Three."
He turns away.

Hattie's rocking
like a rabbi.

The white-browed surgeon
closes the door on the speechless room.

# VI.

Fiends hiss blasphemies
at night.

Lilith twists the tongues of children
at night

Azazel slanders anxious souls
in the wind-whistling night.

# VII.

Fay screams,
"My legs! My legs!"

Her body's
gone rigid.

"O Jesus, my *legs!*"—
are ax-handles,
her backbone
the rod of Moses
striking stone.

Her shoes shake off.
Her legs extend like lengths of wood.
its cushion driving her skirt above
her Nigerian thighs.

Jesus Christ, I *hate* this
unprovided room!

Neither magazines
nor a magazine rack
nor a fake, undusted ficus.
No table, no a bland landscape
nailed to the wall—

just that hollow-mouthed
trashbasket.

I snatch it up.
I upend it.

       *A footstool*
       *against thine enemy.*

I kneel,
and lift her legs,
and set her pink heels
on the basket's
unforthcoming weave.

Cocoa Mary Kingdom
has withdrawn.

I am the Zealot
that despises Rome.

I am Paul
riding to Damascus.

I knead, I knead,
I knead Fay's unyielding muscles
trying to soften them
into a malleable dough,
but failing.

Sweat drips from the tip of my nose,
potting Fay's polished thighs.

But sweat is not
aloe.

Mary Kingdom reappears
with that same, stiff nurse
who halts in the doorway
and glares at my ministrations
like a hawk perched on a post.

"Back off!"
Her voice is a scree.
"I'll take it from here."

"No, you will *not!*
Fay Hopson is *mine!*"

*Ta-tock-a, ta-tock-a!*
Her combat boots
recede like rifle-shots.

# VIII.

What had been Fay's
is mine.
My muscles have taken
her aching in.

She sighs.
Her breath is the wind
of the Spirit.

> *In returning and rest.*
> *In quietness and confidence.*

Fay's hips flex.
She pushes herself up
and leans against the back of the couch.
She crooks her knees,
and gathers her legs up under
the nimbus of her skirt,

"Pastor," saying,
"it guilts me," saying,
"me yellin' at you."

# IX.

My sisters are the Three Saints
who waited in a cave.

In the night the Spirit
plays his penny whistle
across the mouth of the cave.

# X.

The night has clocked to four a.m.
when the impassive surgeon returns
and utters in a flat-toned formality,

"If you wish to see Mr. Hopson,
best do it now."

# XI.

We are four Jacobs, that patriarch
who walked to Rachel's tomb
with a loop of scarlet thread.

We are four King Davids,
weeping psalms over Jonathan's grave.

The Hopson women
are Mary and Mary and Salome,
bringing myrrh and bdellium
to cover the stench of corruption.

No,
they are three uncertain travelers
wandering down a St. Baptiste corridor.

And I am Leroy Hopson's priest
with his Extremest Unction
in my small black box.

The man lies comatose
on a narrow gurney
under the watch of a gleaming chrome machine
which speaks an Aboriginal language:
its first word, *Click,*
its second word, W*hisss.*

Hattie Banks balls her fist.
The woman is Vesuvius erupting.

"Hell-hooks rip they bellies!"
she curses.
"Brimstones burn they babies' eyes!
Goddamn haints
done lef' ma brother lyin'
*naked!*"

Hattie's anger cracks like a hickory limb.
She claws a green sheet from a pale shelf.
She snaps it open,
then billows it like a pallium
down on Sonny Boy's body.

Under the sheet the man's abdomen
mounts up like Zion.

Fay whispers,
"He swole."

Her uncle's feet
project beyond the fabric,
the soles wood-stained,
shining,
hardened by a lifetime's
walking.

"Uncle," Fay murmurs,
"how you goin' dance,
so gone to fat?"

Leroy's lips droop
as heavy as bananas.
His teeth are rimed yellow,
his half-lidded eyes
turned toward eternity.

A tube has uncoiled
and snaked up his nostril.

Leroy's chest
(click)
expands,
then (whisss)
subsides.

Fay touches her uncle's
rucked big toenail
as wide as a spatula.
"O Uncle Sonny,
I ain't thought to bring the clippers
done always did have to home."

Now let Leroy James Hopson's priest
ascend to the head of his bier.

I lean my face close to his,
inhaling (whisss) his fetid exhalations.

"Mr. Hopson,
your family is here to sit vigil."

The sainted Mary Kingdom
floats forward
to keep me company.

"Fay," I say,
"you come too."

Hattie's explosive curse
threw her black wig to the floor.
Pity the old woman's scalp,
scanted with a few grey,
bewildered hairs.

"Leroy James, I've come
to communion you"—
to grant the man
his viaticum.

To that end I unlatch my box.
A tiny paten on his chest,
and a tiny grail
at the foot of Mount Zion.

"Fay? Please, child,
come stand with us."

"I think he dead."

"Nevertheless."

How proud I am of my little sister,
moving so meekly forward.

Leroy's teeth can't chew.
His throat won't swallow.

I break off a fleck of the wafer,
pinch it between my fingernails,
and dip it in the wine.

The morsel sticks
to the pad of my forefinger.

I touch holiness
to Leroy Hopson's tongue.

"This is my body."
    *Click.*
"This is my blood."
    *Whisss.*

Oh, how I wish he would smile,
that dapper little man
in his cream-white suit.

Sing and say,
"Lord, now let your servant
depart in peace. . . ."